VOLKSWAGEN
Beetle

WILLIAM BURT

MBI Publishing Company

About the Author

William Burt was born in the great state of Alabama in September, 1963. After college (Auburn University and Millsaps College) and a brief career with Goodyear, he worked in a precision foundry and machine shop that supplied engineering services and critical, custom-designed, metal components. Their performance-oriented customers ranged from major automotive companies to NASA. His involvement with the engineering side of automotive performance and amateur careers ranging from dirt bikes to auto restoration are responsible for his avid interest and appreciation for anything mechanical. More of an enthusiast than an authority, William has entertained readers on subjects ranging from racecars to tugboats.

First published in 2002 by MBI Publishing Company, Galtier Plaza, Suite 200, 380 Jackson Street, St. Paul, MN 55101-3885 USA

MBI Publishing Company books are also available at discounts in bulk quantity for industrial or sales-promotional use. For details write to Special Sales Manager at Motorbooks International Wholesalers & Distributors, Galtier Plaza, Suite 200, 380 Jackson Street, St. Paul, MN 55101-3885 USA.

Library of Congress Cataloging-in-Publication Data

ISBN 0-7603-1078-5

On the cover:
For over half a century Volkswagen Bugs have provided inexpensive, reliable transportation for the masses. Perhaps no other car has combined availability and style as well as the Bug. From the New Bug to decades-old cars, the roads of the world continue to be traveled by Volkswagen Bugs. *Kathy Jacobs*

On the frontispiece:
The stark design of the New Beetle interior is very pleasant to the eye. Gauges and indicator lights are all located in this compact information center. *William Burt—Buster Miles Chevrolet*

On the title page:
The Bug's popularity ensured that millions of the cars would remain on the road for decades. It also led to the resurrection of the car in the mid-1990s when the "New Beetle" was introduced. *Kathy Jacobs*

On the back cover (top):
This 1964 model Beetle features the bigger windshield and windows that were introduced that year. *Kathy Jacobs*

On the back cover (bottom):
The New Beetle is just as much of a platform for self-expression as the old Beetle.

Edited by Peter Bodensteiner
Designed by Kou Lor

Printed in China

CONTENTS

TO THE READER

This book is an attempt to provide a general overview of the history, engineering, and popularity of the one-and-only Volkswagen Beetle. In such a small format, it is not possible to include all the myriad facts pertaining to the Beetle, so I have concentrated on more significant facts and occurrences. As the Beetle is such a popular subject, however, many useful books, magazines, and VW-focused companies can provide almost any fact. The following books were quite valuable to me as I researched the Beetle, and they offer very detailed information.

VW Beetle
Jonathan Wood, MBI Publishing

Original VW Beetle
Laurence Meredith, Bay View Books

The New Beetle
Matt DeLorenzo, MBI Publishing

Volkswagen Customs & Classics
David A. Fetherston, MBI Publishing

Custom Beetle
Mike Key, Osprey Automotive

The Beetle
Hans-Rüdiger Etzold, Haynes Publishing

Automotive loyalty is a funny thing. Styling and performance excite our automotive pleasure center, but for most of us, our love of big engines and sleek bodies is tempered by budget. In my dreams, my simple gravel driveway is adorned with everything from Duesenbergs to Ferraris. Alas, my financial position forces me to survive on hamburger while dreaming of steak.

America's love affair with power and style started after World War II, when automobiles became more available to the entire population. Mass-produced automobiles were at the height of styling and power in the 1950s and 1960s, especially in the United States. The major American manufacturers changed the styling of their models every year. Power options ranged from mild straight-sixes to huge, fire-breathing V-8s. By the mid- to late 1960s the roads of America were adorned with cars of every shape—with horsepower outputs that ranged from 100 to 600. Manufacturers often reduced the published horsepower ratings in their cars' documentation, hoping to earn lower insurance ratings for their cars. Gas was cheap, America was mobile, and the automobile had arrived as a form of

By the time this car was made in 1974, the combined worldwide production of Beetles was at 2,600 per day. *Volkswagen of America*

self-expression. For most in America, self-expression meant lots of room in the interior and power under the hood.

So how did the Volkswagen Beetle, the most unlikely of candidates, become the most popular automobile in history? At the height of the styling and horsepower wars, a small, insignificant David (a foreign David from Germany, no less) would play a major role in setting Goliath—the Detroit manufacturing community—on its rear.

The car was small, cramped for anyone of size, rather ugly in a cute sort of way, and noisy. Then there was the car's performance. The car handled poorly, but at least this was disguised because it was so slow. So terribly slow. So incredibly, terribly slow. In a day when you could buy an inexpensive big-block Mustang that could compress your spine with a push of your right foot, a ride in a VW Bug was an exercise in patience. If you hit a stretch of road with a stop sign at every block, you could be there all day. And God forbid you should hit a stretch of road with a stop sign at every block that was uphill.

As if that was not enough, the Beetle was brought into existence with the support of none

Top
Possibly the greatest benefit of becoming a Bug enthusiast is the fun-loving community surrounding the car. It is made up of friendly, knowledgeable, and, well, we'll just say "pleasantly strange" people. Every weekend there is a show, rally, or cruise arranged by one of the hundreds of clubs and associations throughout the country.

Right
The Volkswagen Beetle was a "chicken-in-every-pot" kind of car. Its strength was not in speed, handling, luxury, or beauty. Its best attributes were simplicity and volume. As a result, the roads are still adorned with seemingly countless Beetles, and the junkyards are full of Beetles waiting for a chance at a second life.

other than Adolf Hitler. So how in the world did this seemingly doomed automotive platform do it?

Even though the car was small, slow, and ugly, it did have a couple of things going for it: simplicity and timing. Simplicity meant that the car could be produced and sold at a low price, and that it was less likely to break. If it did break, it could be repaired easily and cheaply, often by the owner. And, the car had impeccable market timing. More than once the Bug was sitting ready and waiting when a culture needed exactly what it had to offer. After World War II, Germany, and indeed much of Europe, was in shambles, and the financial position of most of the population was bleak. Many countries needed a simple, inexpensive form of personal transportation while rebuilding after the war. The Bug was there. And, again in the 1960s, when many in the American culture were turning to lifestyles and forms of expression not in accord with the establishment, the Bug was waiting. When fuel consumption became a concern, the Bug's miserly use of gasoline led many to abandon their big gas-guzzlers and pick the tried-and-true German design over the relatively new Japanese small cars. Even after emissions and safety requirements forced the Bug out of the new

With so many Beetles produced by Volkswagen, the world is full of parts, secondhand and new aftermarket. The quest to find the correct part for a car can be one of the more entertaining aspects of antique Beetle ownership.

car showrooms in America, it continued its success in South America. With production shifted to Mexico, the Bug continued to fill the familiar need for inexpensive transportation, as it had in postwar Germany.

Years after being, for all intents and purposes, extinct in the American market, the original Bug still adorns our roads. It is not possible to drive far without seeing a Bug puttering down the road or sitting in a driveway. This fact did not go unnoticed by Volkswagen when it reintroduced the car—albeit much-changed—in the 1990s.

Volkswagen produced more than 21 million Beetles in factories all over the globe. Dollar for dollar, it is arguably the best piece of personal transportation ever built. The car was fun, reliable, and simple, and it could be bought for very little money. And the Beetle was honest. Automobile manufacturers have a record of making inflated claims about their cars. Volkswagen didn't try to do this. It didn't need to.

The Bug was once again a fixture on the car lots and roads of America by 2000. *William Burt—Buster Miles Chevrolet*

1

Creation

THE BIRTH OF THE BUG

It's hard to believe that one of the world's most popular cars had the roots of its creation planted deep in Nazi soil. The car that would become tremendously popular in the United States, Europe, Asia, and South America was originally a dream of Adolf Hitler, and was pushed into production as a part of the National Socialist philosophy. The Beetle was built to be a population-pleasing, "chicken-in-every-pot" platform providing the German people cheap and individually owned transportation.

Keep in mind that there was a time when not everyone over the age of 16 had his or her own car. In fact, most families in both America and Europe did not own a car. In the early years of the automobile, a car was an expensive luxury, especially in Europe. In the 1920s and 1930s, most Europeans living in the countryside still relied on the horse, while those in the city walked or took public transportation. The car was not perceived as a necessity of life, and for longer trips, the train was the preferred mode of travel.

Dr. Ferdinand Porsche started his own design firm in the early 1930s and one of his early designs would become the Beetle. This simple, easy-to-manufacture car would ultimately be credited by many as being the first Beetle design. Before the car went out of production, more than 20,000,000 would be sold in just about every country in the world. *Kathy Jacobs*

The United States was ahead of the world in individually owned transportation because of the Model T. Henry Ford's unique concepts of engineering and production had put car ownership within the financial reach of a large percentage of Americans. But in a time when American production was soaring, Germany was in a depression. When World War I ended in 1918, it left the German economy crippled. The cost of the war and the Treaty of Versailles had driven the country to disaster. Germans scrambling for food and shelter had little time to consider the luxury of an automobile.

Germany would attempt recovery after World War I, and the concept of the Beetle would be a part of the effort. The problem was that the German people hitched their wagon to one of the world's worst. They would shortly begin World War II, again destroying their country and dooming themselves to ruin. But between the two wars, a brief period allowed the Beetle to be designed and created. The idea of the Beetle made it to fruition, but in a way that its creators could never have imagined.

Adolf Hitler became chancellor of Germany in 1933 with a dream of making Germany the most powerful European country. He launched projects that would illustrate to the world Germany's advanced status in science, industry, and technology. One of the projects Germany undertook was the construction of super highways, called autobahns. These were much like the modern American interstate system, which was not begun until the Eisenhower administration. The problem surrounding the idea of the autobahn was not the road itself but the shortage of automobiles. In Germany, automobiles were only for the rich, and there were few of them. If autobahns were built, very few cars would be traveling on them. Logic dictated the need for a car that would be affordable to the masses to fill the great new highway system. Hence the concept of a reliable vehicle that anyone could afford: a people's car.

In the mid-1930s, Beetle prototypes were being tested. The new model was designated the VW3 Series. *Volkswagen of America*

13

During World War II, Volkswagen produced a number of significant military vehicles. Two were the *Kubelwagen* and the *Schwimmwagen*. The Kubelwagen was the German equivalent of the American jeep, although it did not benefit from four-wheel drive. This example is a Type 82 model from around 1943. The interior shot is from a 1944 model. The Schwimmwagen (right) was basically a Kubelwagen with amphibious capabilities. Because it could cross rivers or lakes when traveling cross-country, it made an excellent platform for commandos and reconnaissance. This Schwimmwagen was built in 1942.

In 1934, Hitler personally defined the design specifications for "the people's car." The machine had to be capable of achieving a top speed of 80 kilometers per hour (about 50 miles per hour). It would also be required to have a fuel consumption of 4–5 liters per 100 kilometers (46–58 miles per gallon). To top it all off, the car had to cost the buyer less than 1,000 marks.

In general, the senior executives of the German automobile industry did not think that the car was possible. Their minds were not tuned to an inexpensive, very basic car, and they really didn't care. They were content to produce fewer, more expensive cars for the more affluent. The masses could walk, get a horse, or ride the bus. Profit was their motive, and the specifications for the people's car, especially

the selling price, made profit a questionable issue. Because of this attitude, the German government took charge and invited independent designers to produce and submit designs. One of these contractors was a little-known designer named Dr. Ferdinand Porsche, who already had designed such a "people's car."

Before starting his own company, Ferdinand Porsche had produced designs for both Auto Union and Daimler-Benz, two of the most respected European automobile manufacturers. After leaving these companies, he opened his own design firm in the early 1930s. It was during this time that Dr. Porsche designed the car called the Project 12. The Project 12 was a small, lightweight car that utilized a unit body design. Instead of the body being

15

After the war, the factory would quit manufacturing military vehicles, pull out the old blueprints, and go back to civilian designs. Within a decade, the Wolfsburg factory would be well on its feet and growing rapidly. Production went from 8,987 cars in 1947 to 151,323 in 1953. *Volkswagen of America*

produced separately and mounted on a frame (the preferred manufacturing technique of the times), the body would provide the strength customarily supplied by the frame. The design would save a great deal of weight, which would improve performance. Decades later, the unit body design would take over the world of passenger cars. The Project 12's engine, a small air-cooled model, would be located in the rear of the car. Most scholars of the Volkswagen agree that the Project 12 was the genesis of the Beetle's design.

The Project 12 also attracted the attention of the German automobile manufacturers association,

which financed the design studies for a people's car. The companies that were so reluctant to pursue the idea of a people's car would indirectly finance its design and creation. Porsche, still struggling to start his new firm, gladly accepted the job, but he could not move very quickly as his "design facility" was basically the garage at his house. (It is fitting, given the Bug's personality, that it was born in a home garage.) Despite the problems of being such a small operation, by late 1937, Porsche had built three prototypes of the new car and had put a total of about 100,000 miles on the three. The German auto industry, still not enthusiastic about the car, remained indifferent.

Throughout the Beetle's life, power would be provided by a simple, air-cooled engine. While the motor would be constantly improved, the basic design would remain in production for decades. *Kathy Jacobs*

Hitler, tired of the private manufacturers' foot dragging, decided the government should continue developing the car. He also changed the financing again. Now Hitler would pay for the project with funds from a Nazi-controlled labor party, the *Kraft durch Freude* fund, financed through deductions from German workers' pay. *Kraft durch Freude* translates to "Strength through Joy," hence the tag KdF-wagen. The German government also began a program in which German workers were able to pay five marks a week toward the purchase of one of the new cars. By the end of World War II, more than a quarter-million Germans had signed up for the program. They would never see their cars—the 67 million marks collected from workers for Bugs was seized by the Russians at the end of the war.

Germany publicized the development of the new car, and in 1938, *The New York Times* called the car the "Beetle," for obvious reasons. It was a name that would stay with the car forever.

Despite the start of World War II on September 1, 1938, the first Beetle rolled off the assembly line less than a year later, on August 15, 1940. Production continued throughout the war, but with most resources going to defense factories, Beetle production was meager. By late 1944, Allied bombing had heavily damaged the factory and stopped production. Although Germany did manage to produce 630 cars, few public citizens received them, as most went to Nazi officials. In fact, two of the first Beetle owners were Adolf Hitler and Hermann Goering.

For Germany, World War II ended on May 8, 1945, with the country occupied by American, British, and Russian soldiers, and its population crippled. While euphoria reigned because of the war's end, much of Europe, and practically all of Germany, was in ruins. Most of her cities and industrial areas were completely bombed out and destroyed. At the war's end, the country was split

Next Page
By 1950, Volkswagen had begun manufacturing the Bus. Underneath their vastly different body shells, the Bug and the Bus were very similar mechanically. *Volkswagen of America*

The Beetle would always be a simple machine, but there has always been an artistic element to its simplicity. While the car could never be called extravagant, it was elegant in its own way. *Kathy Jacobs*

into East Germany, controlled by the Soviet Union, and West Germany, controlled primarily by the Americans and the British. The allied victors would not continue to punish West Germany, but would work quickly to build her back up. The Bug would again play an important role in West Germany's resurrection. East Germany would suffer a crueler fate.

Immediately after the war, Germany was divided into four zones of occupation. What was left of the Bug's production plant at Wolfsburg was under British control. A workforce, primarily prisoners of war, began cleaning up and rebuilding. Many of the first cars produced were hybrids, made from available parts, and some of these had a saloon body mounted on a *Kubelwagen* chassis. The Kubelwagen, which greatly resembled the later VW Thing, was a two-wheel-drive military vehicle used by the German army much as the Allies used the jeep. Bugs built on Kubelwagen chassis are easily recognized, as they sit much higher off the ground than the standard model.

One of the more interesting problems associated with the first Bugs produced after the war was the fish smell. The interior trim of the cars was assembled using glue made from fish renderings. The result was an interior that, especially on a warm day, smelled like an old shrimp boat. Combined with an oil cooler that was prone to leak, the car often produced a nauseating smell, which on more than one occasion forced driver and passengers to abandon ship.

Even with the problems, the plant in Wolfsburg was operational by the second half of 1945, and the occupation armies ordered 5,000 cars. Again, the public would have to wait, as these cars were for the occupying military forces. A few cars, however, were diverted for use by the German postal service.

It was a difficult time for both the factory and the country. Employees had to scramble to throw the first few cars together with whatever parts that they had on hand. By the end of 1945, only 58 Bugs had been built, although another 703 saloon-type cars were built by joining a saloon body onto a Kubelwagen chassis. The cars of 1945 came in few colors. Some carried standard British military tan,

others flat black. The Royal Air Force used flat blue; the American forces favored flat gray. A few cars ordered by the Russians were painted flat maroon. The first postwar production cars had 1,131-cc engines, which were originally intended for the *Schwimmwagen*, an amphibious version of the Kubelwagen. The air-cooled engine featured four cylinders, overhead valves, a vertically split crankcase, and hemispherical combustion chambers. Valve size was 28.6 millimeters for both exhaust and intake. The motor had flat top pistons with three rings (two compression and one oil ring), forged rods, and an oil cooler complete with a cooling fan, which rotated at twice the engine speed. Fuel was delivered from a rectangular 8.8-gallon fuel tank through a simple single-barrel carburetor. The first carburetors were manufactured by the Volkswagen factory because of war damage to the Solex plant, which later took over carburetor supply. The engine ran 5.8:1 compression and produced a staggering 25 horsepower at 3,300 rpm. Power was delivered to the wheels by means of a four-speed manual transmission with an 80-millimeter single (dry) clutch. The early cars had cable-operated drum brakes. Hydraulic brakes would not be introduced until the 1950 export model.

In 1946 the production line built up speed, overcoming some of the problems of 1945. By October 1946 the factory had produced its 10,000th unit. Any production in Germany was quite a feat, considering the incredible shortage of every raw material, from rubber to steel. Many of the 1946 Bugs were unique, with headliners, door panels, and seat fabric made from whatever material could be scrounged. Circumstances dictated that few engineering changes were made to the Bug. Simply maintaining production was a full-time job.

In 1947 production dropped slightly from the previous year, with 8,987 cars built. Germany was slowly beginning to get back on its feet, and for the first time, the Bug was offered to the general public. The Bug also began to cross borders, with 56 cars exported to the Netherlands in VW's first official export deal. It was also in 1947 that John Colborne-Baber took a second-hand model, fell in

Volkswagen's Concept 1
As introduced at the 1994 North American
International Auto Show in Detroit, Mich.

More than 60 years after the original Bug came to life, Volkswagen took a second shot at the Beetle. Mechanically the car would be as different from the original Beetle as night from day, but emotionally it was the same in many ways. *Volkswagen of America*

love with it, and became the first United Kingdom dealer, importing and selling used Bugs. Irishman Stephen O'Flaherty got the first official UK import license for new Bugs.

The factory made a few modest changes 1947, establishing a pattern that would remain throughout the Bug's life. Instead of sweeping changes, the factory would continually "tweak" the Bug, making small changes yearly. In 1947 the cars were fitted with chrome—rather than painted—bumpers and hubcaps. Better ball bearings were used in the rear hubs, and a bracket was added to chain and lock the spare tire. The fan housing was improved, with an adjustable flap that could be set for winter or summer, for better engine cooling. On these cars the chassis number was stamped between the handbrake and gearshift.

Another first in 1947 was the appearance of the Bug in America. The first units were not imported by the factory, but instead were brought across the Atlantic by a few enterprising soldiers who could not part with their Bugs when they came home after the war.

In 1948 the year's production would ramp up to 19,244, and the registered company headquarters was moved from Berlin to Wolfsburg. Also in 1948 the first new Bug was brought to the United States by a Dutch importer named Ben Pon. But America was not yet ready for the Bug. American automobile production was just getting reestablished after four years of a war economy, and the American consumer was more likely to purchase a big, powerful American car than the small, underpowered German Bug. But the Wolfsburg factory marched on, and in 1948 the total lifetime production reached 25,000.

One of the biggest moments in the Bug's history occurred in 1948, and it had nothing to do with the mechanics of the car. That was when Heinz Nordhoff came to VW. Nordhoff had been Opel's general manager, and he was not especially fond of the early VW. Nordhoff knew that as times got better, the Bug would have to become more refined and more reliable, or it would become extinct.

The factory would not wait long to begin its process of constant improvement. The dimensions of the 1949 Bug remained the same, but the cars looked better with gloss paint offered in many colors. The body was highlighted with contrasting moldings, while chrome headlight rims, door handles, hubcaps, and bumpers were reshaped and made more aesthetically pleasing. The hood-opening cable was reengineered, and the hood (actually the trunk) could now be opened from inside the car. For driver comfort, the car also had better soundproofing and adjustable-tilt seats. As with many vehicles around the world in the late 1940s, the hole for the handcrank starter disappeared.

In 1949, Volkswagen kept up the pace, producing 46,146 units. On May 13, 1949, the 50,000th Volkswagen was produced, and on July 1, the "export model," a bit more refined than the home version, was introduced. Export models had high-gloss paint, hubcaps, chrome bumpers, headlight rims, and door handles. Although a radio was not offered as an option, the factory made provisions so one could be installed without cutting the sheetmetal dash. Interior appointments for the export model were slightly more refined, and midway through 1949, the seats became more adjustable.

In 1949 a cabriolet designed by the auto body builder Karmann of Osnabruck was also introduced. The car weighed 200 pounds more than the regular model, which further stressed the small air-cooled engine. Ben Pon tried to find garages in America that would be interested in selling Bugs for the factory, but he found no takers. Ben Pon's failure to invade the American market notwithstanding, as the 1940s ended, the Bug faced a bright future. Production was holding its own, material shortages were easing up, and the factory was beginning to refine the car. The Bug had been born during a period of dreams for the German people. Before it could fulfill its role as the people's car, it had been forced to survive a war and the downfall of the system that created it. Although the Third Reich failed, its people's car—its *Volkswagen*—would succeed. In a touch of irony, one of Hitler's dreams would survive as an integral part of Germany's rebuilding and reentry into the world economy.

23

2

Penetration

THE BUG ENTERS THE U.S. MARKET

As the 1950s began, the long-term success of the Bug was far from ensured. Germans bought the Bug in the late 1940s and early 1950s for basic transportation. Although they usually wanted more luxurious and powerful automobiles, there were very few purchasing options, and only the fortunate had any type of car. For the Germans, the Bug was a necessary evil. It would be years before the German roads would be filled with the exceptional cars produced by giants like BMW and Mercedes. When rebuilding a manufacturing economy, plants, machinery, and tooling must all take precedence over consumer products. During this rebuilding, the Bug remained one of the few transportation options for the German people.

In America, the Bug will be remembered as a fun part of youth and a symbol of independence and good times, but in Germany it is more often associated with lean and hard times. This difference in perception would threaten the survival of the first Bug and the creation of the second Bug almost 50 years later.

In 1956 the factory began work on the second million Beetles. While this 1956 model looked much like the car that came a decade before, it was more refined. By 1956 improvements to many of the car's subsystems made it more reliable and user-friendly. *Kathy Jacobs*

By 1952 yearly production had passed the 100,000-per-year mark, and the factory was beginning to make some major improvements to the car. This unique assembly carousel could spit out 240 Bug rear sections each hour. *Volkswagen of America*

In the early 1950s the Bugs that were heading for the export market received most of the engineering improvements. One of the biggest of these was the introduction of hydraulic brakes on the export model. (The standard domestic model still had cable-activated brakes.) In 1950 other minor improvements included better interior ventilation, aided by a cutout in the windows. Ventilation was also improved with opening rear side windows and a cloth sunroof. Nordhoff was beginning to ramp up production of the Bug. In 1950 81,979 Bugs were produced, which brought the total production since its inception to over 100,000 cars. While European sales of the Bug were growing, in the United States, they were only beginning. A meager 157 new Bugs were sold in the United States in 1950.

Another attempt to improve airflow to the passengers was made in 1951 when ventilation vents were put in the front quarters of the body, just in front of the door. Although the Volkswagen engineers had good intentions, these vents "over-improved" passenger ventilation, as they tended to blast too much air in the interior. They were discontinued in 1952. Other small improvements

A Volkswagen can go forward

and backward.

It can go fast

or slow.

It can go uphill,

downhill

and turn around.

Isn't that wonderful?

In 1951, Volkswagen made an attempt to sell the Beetle in the United States. The results were not impressive, as VW sold only 390 cars. In later years, Volkswagen found greater success, partially a result of a lighthearted advertising approach, which captured the fun of Bug ownership. The Volkswagen ad campaign in America was as unique as the car itself. *Volkswagen of America*

continued to appear on the Bug, such as "bright" trim around the windshield in 1951 when sun visors became an option.

By 1952 the factory was finally in a position to make a number of changes to improve the car. Bright molding around the side windows followed the windshield trim of 1951. The window cutouts, which appeared in 1950, were dropped. Opening quarter vent windows were added, however. The car also received a new dash design, and the turn signal was moved from the center of the dash to the steering column. Not all the changes were cosmetic. Mechanically, the car benefited from a new transmission and a better Solex carburetor, which for the first time on a Bug was fitted with accelerator pump and pump jet, which made the engine run more smoothly throughout the powerband.

Ugly is only skin-deep.

It may not be much to look at. But beneath that humble exterior beats an air-cooled engine. It won't boil over and ruin your piston rings. It won't freeze over and ruin your life. It's in the back of the car for better traction in snow and sand. And it will give you about 27 miles to a gallon of gas.

After a while you get to like so much about the VW, you even get to like what it looks like.

You find that there's enough legroom for almost anybody's legs. Enough headroom for almost anybody's head. With a hat

on it. Snug-fitting bucket seats. Doors that close so well you can hardly close them. (They're so airtight, it's better to open the window a crack first.)

Those plain, unglamorous wheels are each suspended independently. So when a bump makes one wheel bounce, the bounce doesn't make the other wheel bump. It's things like that you pay the $XXXX* for, when you buy a VW. The ugliness doesn't add a thing to the cost of the car.

That's the beauty of it.

While the car was being constantly improved, it was still focused more on function than comfort. The interior was very basic, providing driver and passenger with the bare necessities. Items such as locking seatbacks and fuel gauges were still years away. *Kathy Jacobs*

The 1952 changes were successful, and Volkswagen kept the improvements coming in 1953, never resting on its laurels. The Bug became more aesthetically pleasing when color choices grew to include black, pastel green, chestnut brown, Atlantic green, Sahara beige, and metal blue. A milestone change for the Bug occurred on March 10, 1953, when the production line changed from the split rear window to the oval rear window. While collectors now covet the split window cars, many at the time welcomed the improved visibility.

It was during this period that the Volkswagen was becoming a truly international machine. Cars were being exported to many European countries, including Great Britain, and the United States. The success of the export market was varied. While the car was enjoying success in Europe, for a number of reasons the Bug was not yet catching on in America. Gasoline was cheap in the United States, and the American consumer was quite used to large, spacious cars with much more power than the air-cooled Bug. After all, when you looked under a Bug's front hood, there was only a spare tire—a strange experience for most Americans. But with the domestic and export markets combined, the car was becoming a great success for Volkswagen. Production numbers were continuing to rise, hitting 93,709 units in 1951. In 1952 the yearly production broke the 100,000-unit mark, ending up at 114,348 cars. By 1953 production had reached 151,323 cars. Over this three-year period, only 1,971 of these Bugs were sold in the United States (390 in 1951, 601 in 1952, and 980 in 1953).

As 1954 rolled around it was announced that the major body change of 1953 (the new rear window) would be followed by a major engine change for the 1954 model year. In fact, it was the first major engine change since Bug production began. The displacement of the small air-cooled engine grew from 1,131 cc to 1,192 cc. (To put it in perspective, 1,192 cc is 72.74 ci.) The engine was still classified as small, just not as small. The increased displacement was accompanied by an increase in compression, from 5.8:1 to 6.1:1, which also increased power. Compression was later raised to 6.6:1. The valve size for both intake and exhaust was increased from 28.6 millimeters to 30 millimeters. A vacuum advance was also added to the distributor. The result of all of these changes was an increase in power output from 25 to 30 horsepower. True, it was only a 5 horsepower increase, which sounds small in these days of 200-horsepower factory engines. But it was a 20 percent increase from one model year to the next, which is pretty stout. However, this would not solve one of the major problems with the Bug, especially in America. Even with the additional 20 percent, the car was still perceived as horribly underpowered. Another change that brought the car "up to the times" was eliminating the starter button, replaced in 1954 with a key-type starter switch.

Production for 1954 again grew by leaps and bounds, to 202,174 cars, and the export market was getting better. In 1954 a total of 6,343 Bugs were sold in the United States. In 1955 this number would shoot up to 32,662 cars. On August 5, 1955, the Volkswagen production facility reached a milestone when it produced the one-millionth Bug. In only 10 years the factory had evolved from ruin to great prosperity.

Volkswagen continued its process of making minor changes to the Bug every year, and in the mid-1950s, many of these modifications were made to accommodate the new export markets. One change made especially for the United States was a heavier bumper with higher appendages. The export model also featured two chrome exhaust tips instead of one. Other changes for 1955 included a reshaping of the gas tank to increase luggage space. Metal stays were added to keep the doors from opening too far, replacing the cloth stays, which were prone to wearing out. "Eyelids" were added over front lights, which were aesthetically pleasing but really hurt the car's aerodynamic efficiency and slowed it noticeably. With the small engine of the Bug, any aerodynamic disadvantage penalized the car's performance a great deal, much like a modern Winston Cup car racing with a restrictor plate. Another helpful change for maintenance was when the dynamo nut was made the same size as the spark plugs, so one tool could change both. The factory produced 77,812 more Bugs in 1955 than it did in 1954, and by year's end had manufactured 279,986 Bugs.

Volkswagen made few changes to the 1956 Bug, but the few that did occur were significant. Manufacturing quality, after 10 years of production refinement, was very, very good. Americans still knew the Bug as a funny-looking car with a small engine, but a *high-quality* funny-looking car with a small engine. One significant change in 1956 was the introduction of tubeless tires, which by year's end had been mounted on 800 production vehicles. Another was an alloy change in the timing gear, which ensured much less wear over time.

In 1957, VW made a major production scheduling change, running the model years from August to August instead of by the calendar year. In a landmark design change, at the end of July 1957, chassis number 1-0 600439 came off the assembly line bearing the last oval window. The new rectangular window was almost twice the size and provided

much better rear visibility for the driver. This was the second rear window change that marked a milestone still recognized by collectors. (The first was the disappearance of the split rear window in 1953.) The rear window change necessitated a redesign of the engine air intake area and the engine lid. The driver also got better visibility ahead, as the front windshield was enlarged a bit for the 1957 model. A few noticeable changes were also made to the interior of the car. The dash was again redesigned. Knobs were laid out in a new pattern, the radio was moved, and the glovebox was enlarged. Vinyl door panels replaced the traditional cloth, and the rearview mirror was enlarged to accompany the bigger rear window. The interior received additional soundproofing, especially in the rear. The bad news was that while the heavy wool material worked very well as soundproofing, it retained moisture and tended to rot, stink, and promote rust.

The major changes of 1957 meant few for the 1958 production year, with the focus more on production consistency and quality. And consistency was not the only thing growing on the assembly line. In 1956 the factory ramped up to 333,190 cars; in 1957, to 380,561, and in 1958, Volkswagen pumped out 451,526 cars.

By 1959 the factory was back to its habit of making small changes. Door handles now sported push buttons, and redesigned seats were softer and more curved for better lateral support. And again the interior received more and more soundproofing to fight the Bug's reputation as a very noisy machine. Some improvements were made to the suspension in 1959, which helped to make the Bug a better-handling car. The Bug always had a tendency to oversteer—that is the rear end wanted to "swing out" in a hard turn. Once it got going, it was very difficult, if not impossible, for the driver to get it straight again. The lack of power and force of the weight of the rear-mounted engine usually

The 1956 model was the last year of the small, oval rear window. The rear window was redesigned and enlarged in 1957. *Kathy Jacobs*

Top

While the dash was still simple in 1956, it was aesthetically pleasing, especially with the addition of the wicker storage tray. *Kathy Jacobs*

Left

Power in 1956 was supplied by an 1,192-cc engine, which produced about 30 horsepower. *Kathy Jacobs*

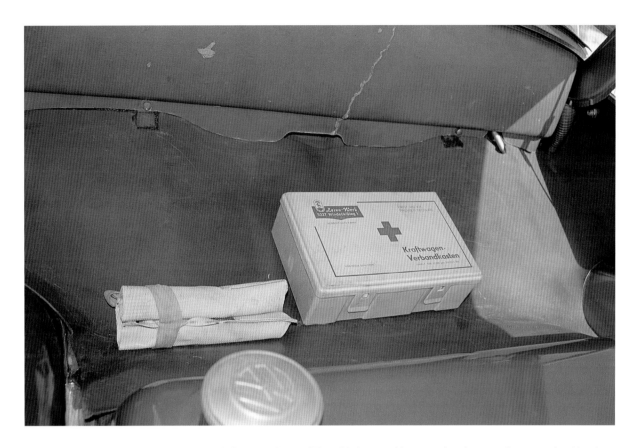

While baggage capacity was limited in the early Bugs, the factory did provide buyers with some unique items, such as a couple of handy tools and a first-aid kit. *Kathy Jacobs*

meant the car would spin—at least once. In 1959 the factory added anti-sway bars, which tightened the link between the car's body and suspension and dramatically decreased the tendency to oversteer. During 1959 the factory reached the incredible rate of 4,000 cars produced per day. Although the bulk of the sales were still coming from outside the United States, part of the increase was due (finally) to increased interest in America.

As the 1950s ended, sales numbers for the Bug really began to climb. The factory had produced a whopping 575,407 cars in 1959, but it would pale in comparison to the 725,927 in 1960 and the 796,825 in 1961. This growth in popularity was accompanied by another growth in power from the

motor. While the 1960 Bug's engine would retain the same displacement, the power would increase from 30 to 34 horsepower, a 13.3% jump, achieved by bumping the compression ratio from 6.6:1 to 7.0:1. Another engine change was welcomed when an automatic choke was added to the carburetor. With a six-volt electrical system, anything that helped the car start better was very welcome. In March, the factory added a steering damper to further improve the car's inherently poor handling, and the fusebox was moved from the luggage area to under the dash. A plastic grab handle was also added for the passenger.

The refinements of 1961 continued to make the Bug more user-friendly and helped bring the

Bug up to industry standards. To help owners and mechanics, the bonnet was now held by a spring-loaded self-supporting assembly. Winter comfort was improved with better heating around the foot level in the rear and adjustable heated airflow in front. Another great driving mystery was solved for Bug owners when, for the first time, a Bug could be purchased with a fuel gauge. While amenities were improving, the overall safety of the Bug was still questionable. The situation was improved somewhat in 1961 when seat-belt anchors were available from the factory, although the belts themselves had to be ordered separately. The Bug's handling was again addressed in 1961 with a new worm and roller steering system.

When the 1962 Bug came out, the body was pretty much the same as the 1961 model. The interior changed a bit when a new vinyl headliner replaced the traditional cloth one. For the second consecutive year, the rear passenger's comfort was addressed, with adjustable heater ducts for rear passenger foot heaters. Late in the 1962 production run, the interior heating system was completely reengineered, a welcome change for the Bug owner. For years, heat had been supplied to the interior of the car by directly piping the dirty exhaust air that had been heated by the engine. The new system would incorporate heat exchangers. With the new system, the hot exhaust gas was piped to the exchanger, where the hot gas heated clean air, which was used to heat the cockpit. The heat exchangers dramatically lessened the likelihood of exhaust fumes entering the passenger area. It is another example of the factory listening to its customers and fixing its mistakes.

Few changes were in store for customers when the 1963 models hit the showroom floor—but there were always one or two. A smaller, sliding metal sunroof was introduced to replace the large cloth rollback type on the export model. Seat covers

Not all of the Beetles roaming America's roads are export models. Private individuals shipped some Beetles from Germany to the United States. This European 1959 model is still a daily driver.

These unique European turn signals, known as semaphores, never appeared on the export model. In their normal position the indicator is recessed into the car's body. When turning, the indicator pops out to indicate the direction of the turn.

followed the previous year's headliner change, becoming vinyl instead of cloth. By the end of 1963 there was a new situation for the factory. In every year since 1947 the Bug's sales had grown, often by huge percentages. In 1962 production peaked at 867,000 units. But when the 1963 numbers were tallied, production had dropped to 839,000 units, a 3.23 percent decrease. Part of the problem was probably that the 1200 model had been around a while. The converted already had one, and were

not likely to buy a new model if it was essentially the same as the one they had.

The Bug was once again about to undergo some pretty major changes. The first came in 1964 with a relatively major body change. Keep in mind that with the Bug's longevity, its major refinements are like minor refinements to other cars. In 1964 the driver received better visibility when the factory once again changed the body to have bigger windows and a slightly curved front windshield,

This Coral 1960 is a good example of how color could set Beetles apart when all cars from many decades looked essentially alike. In an effort to attract buyers throughout the Beetle's life, Volkswagen coated the car with many unique and different colors. *Kathy Jacobs*

Next Page
The convertible body style was always a popular one amoung Beetle enthusiasts. *Kathy Jacobs*

In 1960 power from the small engine went from 30 to 34 horsepower, thanks mainly to an increase in compression. This 1960 was later equipped with dual carburetors to further increase horsepower. *Kathy Jacobs*

which had been flat. The windshield wipers were lengthened to fully cover the new windshield, and the size of the sun visors was increased. Luggage space increased by giving a fold-down feature to the rear seatback.When the back was down, the interior noise was louder but you could certainly carry more stuff.

The body changes of 1964 were followed by a major engine change for 1965. The 1,200-cc engine would still be produced for the base model cars, but the factory introduced a larger 1,300-cc model. The 1,300 (1,285-cc) motor had a longer stroke, increasing from 64 to 69 millimeters. Compression also rose, from a ratio of 7:1 to 7.3:1. The total performance gain for these changes was an increase of 6 horsepower over the 1,200-cc model. The new motor was rated at 40 horsepower at 4,000 rpm, an increase of more than 17 percent.

While this change in no way made the Bug a rocket ship, every little bit did help. The new 1300 was capable of going from 0 to 60 in 23 seconds, with a maximum speed of 76 miles per hour. Both of these performance stats were very low compared to American standards, but relative to the old Bugs, things were getting better. After the major body changes of the previous year, about the only exterior change was when the 1200 emblem was replaced with a 1300 emblem. Even though performance was not up to American standards, the Bug was now a significant seller in the U.S. market. In 1964, VW of America sold more than 236,000 Bugs in the United States.

So in 1965 the refinements continued. One great interior improvement of 1965 was a seat backrest tilt adjuster that would lock, keeping the seatback from flying forward during sudden stops.

On the 1965 model, balljoints replaced king pins and link pins on the front suspension, and more torsion leaves were added. The Bug also came with ventilated road wheels for the first time. These provided for better brake cooling and dropped "unsprung weight," which always provides for a performance gain.

In an uncharacteristic move for Volkswagen, major engine changes occurred in consecutive years. The days of the 1,300-cc engine as king of the Bug motors did not last long. While the Bug was innovative, simple, and unique, it had always had performance drawbacks. The biggest of these was a lack of power, followed closely by poor handling.

The factory would again address both in 1966. The new king of the engines would become the 1500. The bigger displacement motor clocked in at 1,496 cc, and was rated at 44 horsepower at 4,000 rpm with 78 ft-lb of torque at 2,600 rpm. Within the engine, the stroke stayed the same (69 millimeters) as the 1300, but the bore was increased from 77 to 83 millimeters to achieve the new displacement. The engine's compression ratio was again increased, this time from 7.3:1 to 7.5:1. For better top-end performance, the rear gear ratio was dropped from 4.375:1 in the 1300 to 4.125:1 in the 1500. Although more displacement was always welcome, the 1500's electrical system would remain a somewhat antiquated six-volt system.

On the 1500 model, handling was also better. Radial tires were now available, replacing the venerable bias-ply tires. The rear track of the car was also increased, from 1,250 millimeters on the 1200 model to 1,350 millimeters on the 1500 model. Helping slow the car were disc brakes in the front and drum brakes in the rear. The 1300 model would stay with drum brakes all around. The major changes of 1966 would be accompanied by a few small changes, including "easier to reach" seat backrest levers, black control knobs on the dash, and a black steering wheel to help eliminate windshield reflections. The new black knobs were

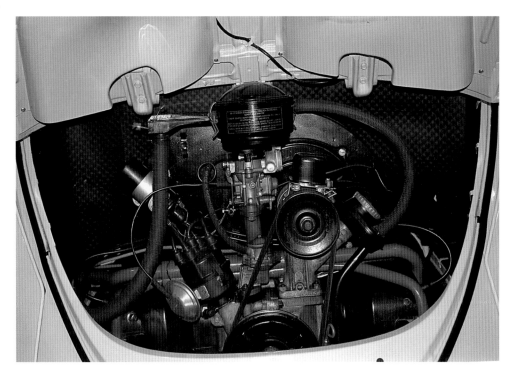

Power for 1962 stayed the same at 34 horsepower. Buyers would have to wait until 1965 when the 40-horsepower engine was introduced.
Kathy Jacobs

Some major body changes were made for the 1964 model year. Among the biggest changes were a bigger windshield and windows, which improved the driver's visibility. *Kathy Jacobs*

In 1964 the rear seat could be folded flat, providing more storage space when only two passengers were in the car. Throughout the car's life, the factory constantly found small ways to make the car better. *Kathy Jacobs*

also made flatter and softer to help eliminate injury during crashes. And for the first time, the driver could use the same key for both the doors and the ignition.

The Bug had arrived in the United States. A youth culture was thinking contrary to the establishment, and automakers would take notice. Cars like Ford's Mustang were built with the youthful customer in mind. Volkswagen would not have to custom-tailor a product for this new buyer.

The Bug's philosophy of understatement, value, and simplicity would fit this new market perfectly, giving the American youth mobility and independence. For the factory the hardest task would not be sales, but supply. However, even as sales were about to peak, changes already under way would sound the death knell for factory sales of the Bug in America. But before emissions controls and safety standards took their toll, the Bug would—in its small way—help to change America.

Completion

THE BUG'S LONG LIFE AND LINGERING DEATH

By the mid-1960s the Bug had been a high-volume production model for 20 years, and during that time it changed very little, especially compared to automobiles manufactured in the United States. Americans tended to like new models every year—look at the difference in Chevrolets from 1955 to 1958. Through four production years, the Chevy bodies changed dramatically. For the Bug, a major change was a dash redesign, a relocated vent, or new colors offered. Fashion, not function, sold the lion's share of the cars in America. So to some degree, the "great coming" of the Bug as a big seller in the United States occurred when "less" became fashionable. Sure, the Bug was affordable to young people, but so were other cars. Most of the time, when car owners picked the Bug as their mode of transportation, they were running counter to the establishment. As the 1960s drew to a close, the Bug was being forced to change because of outside factors dictated primarily by the government. The Bug had been a product of factory design and consumer demand, but this was about to change. Many of the new external changes were the result of uniform safety standards introduced in the United States, which were focused on better driver and passenger safety. In 1967 the Beetle was again fitted with bigger bumpers that were stronger and higher.

The timing of the Beetle was perfect in America. As youth began to think differently from their parents, the Bug was a great choice in transportation for those who wanted to be different. This car, manufactured in 1967, offered three great benefits—it was cheap, fun, and different. *Kathy Jacobs*

Volkswagen's unique construction keeps moisture out.

For years there have been rumors about floating Volkswagens.

Why not?

The bottom of the Volkswagen isn't like ordinary car bottoms. A sheet of flat steel runs underneath the car, sealing the bottom fore and aft.

That's not done to make a bad boat out of it, just a better car. The sealed bottom protects a VW from water, dirt and salt. All the nasty things on the road that eventually eat up a car.

The top part of a Volkswagen is also very seaworthy. It's practically airtight. So airtight that it's hard to close the door without rolling down the window just a little bit.

But there's still one thing to keep in mind if you own a Volkswagen. Even if it could definitely float, it couldn't float indefinitely.

 So drive around the big puddles. Especially if they're big enough to have a name.

46

The Bug was just the right car for the counterculture of the late 60s and early 70s. The car was simple and understated compared to the "standard" large cars of American society. But the Bug also offered its own brand of style, providing owners with both simplicity and fun. *Kathy Jacobs*

In another welcome change, in August 1967 the Bug finally got 12-volt electrical system. Since its introduction, the Bug had used a 6-volt electrical system, and when the battery was in top condition, this system functioned well. But one dead cell in the battery often meant that a power loss was so significant that the car would not crank. With a 12-volt system, one or even two dead cells did not necessarily mean a starting failure. The power of the 12-volt system was a welcome change to all, but especially to those in cold climates. Other changes on the 1967 model included vertical headlights, which were mounted in reshaped front fenders. The fuel filler nozzle was also relocated, so the owner could fill up without opening the hood. At the rear of the 1967 model, the engine lid was

Left
As the 1960s began to draw to a close, the sight of a Bug puttering down the highway had become familiar to most Americans. This visibility, combined with imaginative advertising, helped Beetle sales in America grow by leaps and bounds. *Volkswagen of America*

shortened a bit, and the rear light units were enlarged. For the first time, the rear light units could be purchased with reverse lights as an option. Another exterior change on the 1967 model was to the running board covers—now offered in any color you wanted as long as it was black. The factory had previously matched, or attempted to match, the covers to the body color.

Mechanical changes included an optional innovative new transmission, the semiautomatic three-speed. The car retained the floor-mounted shifter, with a solenoid and a vacuum system that automatically engaged the clutch when the driver shifted gears, eliminating the need for a clutch pedal. While the transmission was innovative and eliminated the clutch, a fearful piece of equipment to those untrained in driving with a manual transmission, in practice the unit was not all that well received as it certainly did nothing to improve the car's performance.

Volkswagen sales received an unexpected boost in 1967 from a strange source. Disney's film *Herbie the Love Bug* starred a racy Bug—complete with personality and self-expression. Herbie was the likable underdog, and America loved him. The Disney film was partly responsible for the continuing strong sales in America, which in 1968 hit about 400,000 units.

From a corporate view, Volkswagen would forever change in early 1968. Heinz Nordhoff, who had been at the wheel of VW manufacturing since 1948, died on April 12, 1968, at the age of 69. For years the Bug's success had come under his leadership. Nordhoff left behind a thriving company, still owing its success to a car the factory had always produced with half-hearted enthusiasm.

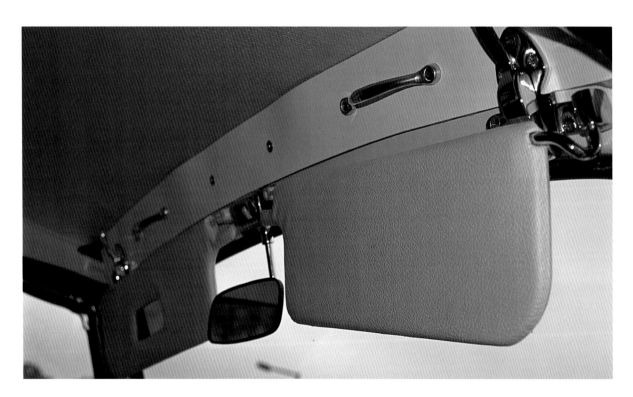

Even at a low sales price, the Beetle was a reliable, quality vehicle. Appointments were basic but were usually well made and would last. *Kathy Jacobs*

In August of 1967, the Beetle buyer was treated to a new electrical system. The long-standing 6-volt system was dropped in favor of a more powerful 12-volt system. More power meant better starting, especially in cold climates.

Sales were climbing. The total number for world production was now more than 1.1 million cars.

At the height of the Beetle's success, critics proclaimed that the car had run its course, especially in America. And it was the same old story. The Bug was simple and ugly, it handled poorly, and it was still terribly slow. Keep in mind that in the late 1960s the buzz in Detroit was about size and power. If a big engine was good, a bigger engine was better. Engines like Ford's 426, Chevy's 427, and Mopar's 440 were being put into both midsized and large cars, from Mustangs to Chargers. American cars were offering accessories such as power steering, power brakes, automatic transmissions, and air conditioning. The Bug was so far removed from Detroit's production philosophy that critics filled column after column with graphic descriptions of the Bug's shortcomings. But in the world of automobile production, the only statistic that really matters is unit sales, providing the model can be sold for more than it costs to produce it. The Bug may have run its course with critics by the mid-1960s, but not with the public.

In 1968 the Volkswagen produced 1,136,134 Bugs. Not bad for a 20-year-old design that wasn't "advanced" to begin with. The 1968 model introduced a few new features, including a collapsible steering column, a lockable fuel cap, and hazard

Next Page
In 1970 the Beetle started its fifth decade, but the new cars were not that different from the first Beetles. This 1970 is a one-owner car that has been driven at least every week since it was purchased.

In 1970 buyers could choose between two engines; the 44-horsepower 1300, or this one, the 50-horsepower 1600.

lights. Disc brakes and the semiautomatic gearbox, previously available only on the 1500 model, were offered on the 1300 model. As the Bug moved into the last year of the 1960s, Volkswagen introduced the "luxury" package in an effort to sell a more "refined" people's car. The special option car was marked with an "L" badge on the engine lid. The luxury package included backup lights, an antiglare rearview mirror, a padded dash, rubber inserts in the bumpers, a lockable glovebox, and deep-pile carpet. The American version also had silver wheels and buzzers to alert passengers to an open door.

In 1970, for the fourth time, production of the car would start in a new decade. The 1970 model initiated one of the biggest changes in Beetle history, when the front suspension changed from torsion bars to struts. Torsion bar suspension is made up of a bar with "arms" attached on each end. These arms are attached to the torsion bar on one side and the suspension on the other. When the car hits a bump in the road, the arm is forced up, twisting the torsion bar and putting spring into the suspension. Torsion bar suspensions were used for years on automobiles and are still very popular on

Interior appointments were still simple but a bit more polished. Safety drove many of the interior changes, as padded dashes and softer knobs helped protect passengers in accidents.

tanks and other tracked, military vehicles. The new MacPherson strut suspension combined the shock and spring into one smaller, lighter unit. Dropping the torsion bar system and adding the MacPherson struts almost doubled the Bug's front luggage space.

On the back of the Bug, the superior, rear double-jointed suspension, introduced on the 1967 semiautomatic-transmission cars, became standard equipment on all models except the basic 1200 and 1300 models. The 1,500-cc engine was dropped from the sales list. Customers could now choose between the 1,300-cc engine that produced 44

Right
Convertibles and ragtops had been available for years, and later a "hard" sunroof became available.

A stroll through a junkyard reveals the biggest suspension change in the Beetle's history. In 1970, torsion bars were replaced with MacPherson struts. The torsion bar suspension (left) relied on a "pretensioned" bar to provide the spring action for the suspension. The torsion bar was replaced with coil springs, which were incorporated in the MacPherson strut.

horsepower and the new 1600, which replaced the 1500. The 1600 engine (actually 1,584 cc) produced 50 horsepower. The new, larger displacement was achieved by increasing the bore to 85.5 millimeters. Both the 1,300-cc and 1,600-cc engines had a new cylinder head, which had two ports per cylinder for better flow. Basically it was still the same old head with an extra hole bored into it. While this did offer more capacity for fuel/air flow,

it presented a new problem. On some heads the removal of the extra material led to cracking of the cylinder head. The new engine was also equipped with an aluminum (instead of steel) oil cooler. The 34-horsepower 1200 engine model would still be manufactured with the single-port heads. While the extra power was seen as a step forward, all changes were not as well received. One infuriating change for the 1970 model was placing the jack

The new MacPherson strut front suspension allowed much more space for luggage.

Next Page
The year 1972 was a big one for the Beetle. It passed the Ford Model T as the most-produced car in the history of the world.

The simple Beetle motor had always been a benefit and selling point, but in the early 1970s the automotive world was changing quickly. Exhaust emission controls were being taken seriously in America, and there was only so much the engineers could do to clean up the air-cooled Bug motor.

under the rear seat, requiring the owner to remove passengers or cargo to change a flat tire.

For the 1971 model, the big changes were expanding rear window height 4 centimeters on the saloon model, and moving the windshield wiper switch from the dashboard to the steering column lever.

On February 17, 1972, total production of the VW Bug passed the magic number of 15,007,033. This may sound like a strange number to be of consequence, but to automobile manufacturers it was the Holy Grail. This number represented the total lifetime production of Henry Ford's Model T. Passing this number made the Bug the most-produced model in automotive history.

In 1972 the Bug again got a new dash. This one was more modern in appearance, and it eliminated the metal fascia on the dashboard. While the new dash was attractive, it did seem to detract from the character of the Bug's interior.

For 1973 the 1200 model received the larger rear lights and bumpers that the other models carried. All Bugs with MacPherson struts were also supplied with a self-stabilizing steering system to

Interior appointments continued to be refined. By 1972 the dash and steering wheel had yet again been redesigned.

help the car track better, and those headed for America now had reinforced bumpers with shock absorbers. VW was forced into this modification because of the new 5-mile per hour bumper standard.

By 1974, Volkswagen was doing everything possible to keep the Beetle legal in America. Every year in the United States, emissions and safety requirements were becoming more strict. These laws hit the Bug especially hard, because of the car's inherent design. Emissions control measures usually have an adverse effect on horsepower, and the Beetle had no horsepower to spare. The car was not in much better shape to meet safety requirements with weight under 2,000 pounds and with the engine in the rear. Cars destined for the

Sales of the Beetle were beginning to lag in the mid-1970s, especially in the United States. The convertibles were still a popular item, though, and few look better than this 1975 yellow Super Beetle. *Kathy Jacobs*

Volkswagen used the basic design of the Beetle to manufacture different cars, giving buyers a greater range of choices. The Karmann-Ghia (above) was the most produced of the "non-Bug models." VW also produced the fastback (right) and the notchback (left). *Kathy Jacobs*

United States were equipped with fuel injection, a catalytic converter, and a smog pump.

In 1974 the last Beetle was made at Germany's Wolfsburg factory. Volkswagen was beginning to put its eggs in different baskets. A year after the May 1973 introduction of the Passat, with its front-wheel drive and four-cylinder water-cooled engine, VW unveiled the Scirocco and the Golf. At Wolfsburg, the assembly line was being changed to produce Golfs. Body and part production for the Bug would continue at Wolfsburg, with the cars themselves produced elsewhere. Worldwide production was 2,600 Bugs a day. In 1974 total cumulative production passed the 18,000,000 mark, but the writing was on the wall.

In 1977 the sale of the hardtop Bug ceased in the United States, while the Cabriolet would be sold until 1980. By 1979 yearly sales of new Bugs dropped to only 2,500 in the United States. As U.S. sales volume shrunk, Volkswagen knew it was not prudent to make expensive changes that had little hope of achieving a payback. Some enthusiasts would bring Mexican Bugs into the country, but these were not traditional "factory sales."

The Bug seemed to be drawing its last breath. In the 1970s production facilities in Germany and

around the world began to close. The Ingolstadt facility had ceased production in 1969. It was followed by the New Zealand facility in 1972. The main plant in Wolfsburg switched production in 1974, and in 1975 the same happened in Hanover. The Belgium plant stopped in 1975, while plants in Portugal, Yugoslavia, and Australia stopped in 1976. Eire stopped in 1977, Emden in 1978, South Africa in 1979, and Osnabruck in 1980. In Africa and South America, Bug production lasted a bit longer. As other facilities were ending production of the Bug in the mid-1970s, a production line began to produce Bugs in Nigeria in 1975 and lasted 14 years, closing in 1989. During the same decade, the Asian production dwindled. Production of Bugs in Thailand and Singapore ceased in 1974 and facilities in Malaysia and Indonesia stopped in 1977. A plant in the Philippines, the last Asian production site, lasted until 1982. Much of the South American production ceased in the 1980s. The Venezuela plant stopped in 1981, the Uruguay plant in 1982, and the plant in Peru in 1987. Production in Brazil lasted over 40 years. The plant that began producing Bugs in 1953 finally ended production in 1996. This left the Mexican production lines as the last manufacturer of Bugs in the world. In 1985 exports of the Bug to Europe ceased. While official importing to America and Europe had ended, more than a few Mexican Bugs made it to both continents.

The Bug's demise was caused as much by the legal requirements of selling a car in America as it was caused by fading popularity. While all must agree on the benefits of better safety and lower pollution, the rise of these laws caused the Bug to disappear from dealer lots. But the little cars would prove resilient. The millions of cars that had been produced would last much longer than their builders could possibly have imagined. And 20 years later, a new platform from Volkswagen would revitalize a huge Bug culture all over the world. Once again the Bug would not die. It would change.

Beetle sales in America in 1979 were only a fraction of what they had once been. In 1968, VW sold about 400,000 Beetles in the United States; in 1979 it sold 2,500, all convertibles. But the 1979 convertible was a nice machine. It had been refined for more than 40 years, and now could be bought with leather seats and fuel injection.

Imagination

AN AUTOMOTIVE PLATFORM OF EXPRESSION

Even though the Bug had left the dealer showrooms, the American psyche had been infected with Bug fever. It still runs rampant. While many enthusiasts favor original cars, others find the Bug the perfect platform for artistic automotive expression. Man has always customized his traveling machine. The first "souped up" machine was probably a fancily carved and decorated walking stick. Later, when the horse was domesticated, it was individualized in every possible way. Native Americans painted them, knights hung brightly covered linens all over them, and cowboys studded saddles with silver.

The automobile would be no different. For years the world had many small automobile manufacturers who primarily sold to the affluent. Each manufacturer offered many custom touches for the driver. But as the mass-produced models began to take over, and the industry moved from a collection of small companies to a few large companies, options for custom autos began to shrink. By the 1960s and 1970s the pool of automobile choices had become so limited that if you wanted some individuality in your car, you pretty much had to do it yourself.

Beetle owners can make enough modifications to improve looks and performance without irreparably damaging their cars' value. *Kathy Jacobs*

The $35,000 Volkswagen.

Have we gone stark raving mad?

No, but when we heard this car was on display at the Los Angeles International Auto Show, we thought somebody had.

As it turned out, there was a method to the owner's madness.

Why not transform the world's best known economy car into the world's most economical limousine?

After all, a lot of the things that make great luxury cars great are already there in the humble little Bug:

Like 23 years of perfecting every single part of the car.

And subjecting it to over 16,000 different inspections before we sell it to you.

And having it worth lots of money to you when you sell it to someone else.

So why not stretch it out to limo length?

Why not add an intercom, bar and mahogany woodwork and tufted English upholstery and a carriage lamp to signal the doorman?

 Why not be the savingest millionaire on the road?

That, children, is exactly how the rich get richer.

Beetle projects can be infinitely tailored to the owner's tastes. This owner needed a small, lightweight car to be pulled behind an RV. The answer is a pretty stock Beetle adorned with the livery of the owner's favorite NASCAR driver, awesome Bill (from Dawsonville) Elliot.

In America everything from sports cars to vans are painted, lowered, stripped, souped up, and mated to the driver's dream. But there has probably never been an automotive platform that offers as many possible ways to individualize as the VW Bug. Of the Bug's many great attributes, one of its biggest is its ability to allow owners to modify and personalize their purchase. While the car has not been sold new in the United States for many years, the supply of factory and aftermarket parts products to improve or distinguish the average Bug is still almost limitless.

Bugs make wonderful dune buggies, cruisers, racers, and novelty cars. And as hobbies go, the Bug lifestyle is filled with friendly people, walking encyclopedias, and good times. Just beware. This group of great people is split between those who enjoy

Left

The factory picked up on their customers' desire to individualize their Bugs. In this advertisement, Volkswagen used a "Limo Bug" that was customized in (where else) Los Angeles. *Volkswagen of America*

Others may leave the Beetle with a stock appearance but will elect to end the "horsepower problem" once and for all. Here a small-block Chevy engine has been shoehorned into the front of a Bug to surprise many "red light-to-red light" opponents.

When building a street cruiser, the Beetle owner has many options and can be just as wild as his or her imagination allows. Color is usually the first decision—it's hard to go wrong with red. *Kathy Jacobs*

seeing different modifications and those who see any deviation from factory specifications as an unholy act. If you are a member of the first group and want to modify a Bug, there are two general paths to follow. Most Bug conversions are either "street cruisers" or "off-road ramblers."

While many platforms offer more power and size, many street cruisers out there are pretty hot. Power can be supplied by "souped up" factory engines or entirely different power plants. Everything from Porsche engines to small-block Chevrolets have been crammed into Bugs. Just about every factory suspension component can be replaced to improve handling or just to change the ride height. Bodies can be stretched, shortened, flared, or chopped. All of the colors of the rainbow have adorned Bugs, and more than one has been painted all of the colors of the rainbow. Interior

No two custom interiors are the same. Seats, dash, and other appointments can be custom-built or replaced with aftermarket products. *Kathy Jacobs*

Originality is great, but anyone can understand the appeal of an engine so clean and dressed-up you can eat off of it. *Kathy Jacobs*

Movies and cartoons made the dune buggy a dream of many American youth. There are few rides as pleasant as a long cruise in a buggy on a warm summer's day. *Kathy Jacobs*

modifications range from the mild, with only the factory fabrics being replaced, to the extreme, with new seats, dashes, and stereos that can explode the unwary passenger's head. Regardless of the owner's choice, the process is endless, and few will ever consider their car finished. One or two touches are always on the drawing board.

If an owner wants to get away from it all, the Bug offers a perfect platform for either a dune buggy or modified off-road vehicle. While the Bug did not have the benefit of four-wheel drive (without major modifications, and rest assured someone

has done it), it did benefit from light weight and great maneuverability. You can proceed one of three basic ways to go from a road Bug to an off-road Bug. The first is to quickly remove the fenders and strip off anything that adds weight without having a purpose—very little on the Bug. With nerf bars replacing bumpers, and a set of aftermarket high-vent exhaust pipes, an owner can have a very decent hunting or camping vehicle with little expense or effort. A second popular conversion approach is to completely ditch the factory body in favor of a true "dune buggy" fiberglass body.

Although rail buggies only have rear-wheel drive, they can go places one would not believe. This is often accomplished by speed instead of traction, which makes being the driver fun and being the passenger terrifying. Big rear tires, high ground clearance and an advantageous horsepower-to-weight ratio mean that hills and streams fade behind the driver, mile after mile.

This conversion is perfect for "light" off-road duty like cruising the desert dunes, coastal beaches, or crowded boulevards. For the greatest off-road performance, the best choice is a rail job. When building a rail, body and chassis are scrapped in favor of a light but strong tube-steel chassis/roll cage. Suspension components, engines, and electrical systems—and not much else—are transferred from the Bug body to the rail. These cars range from the simple, with few improvements from stock, to high-dollar race and recreation machines with custom suspensions and highly modified engines.

Either way you go, off-road or on-road, you'll find a ready supply of aftermarket stock and modified Bug parts. This offers enthusiasts two great advantages—variety and price. With more than 20 million Bugs produced, they will be on the roads for decades, making the production of parts a sound business proposition. The high volume of Bugs also means high production volumes of parts, which helps keep costs and prices down. For all of our lifetimes, we can rest assured that we will continue to see every imaginable Bug concoction cruising the roads of America.

Resurrection

THE NEW BEETLE

It is easy to criticize automotive executives, and if you work on your own car, automotive engineers. By putting yourself in a position of empathy, you might understand some of the difficulties of introducing a new car model. It is a process in which one must really climb out on a limb. With success, all rejoice; with failure, most point fingers. Reintroducing a model can be even more difficult when the buying public has a preconceived image of the old model; if it is being resurrected, chances are that it was a classic, loved by all. This was the advantage and the dilemma when the idea of a new Bug went from fantasy to reality in the 1990s.

Many, many Europeans and Americans have Bug memories. It's hard to find anyone from the age of 30 to 60 who has not either owned a Bug or had a friend who owned one. These memories often include youth, near poverty, free time, close friends, and fun. But memories may also include slow speeds, bad handling, loud interiors, sweltering in the summer without air conditioning, and freezing in the winter with inferior heating. Still, in America the Bug is most often remembered fondly. Europeans may have an entirely different set of memories. The Bug was available to them when little else was; it is the car often associated with the lean times after World War II.

Beetle enthusiasts' prayers were answered in 1998 when they could once again go to a VW dealer and buy a Beetle. For a while this would be a difficult task, however, as demand quickly outpaced supply. As a result, many 1998 Beetles sold for well over sticker price.

75

While the New Beetle was very different in the mechanical sense, it was the same old Beetle when it came to ownership. Just like the original, many New Beetles were individualized by their owners. This New Beetle was adorned with flames shortly after it was bought.

VOLKSWAGEN IN AMERICA: CHRONICLE OF A CAR COMPANY

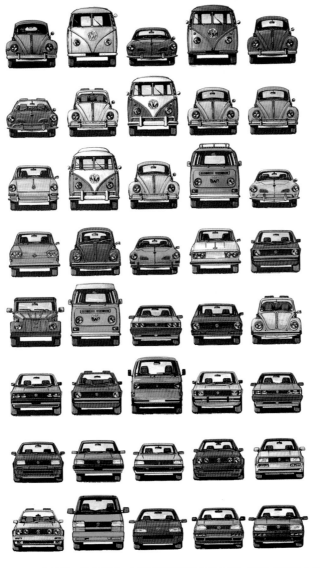

 VOLKSWAGEN 40TH ANNIVERSARY CELEBRATION

VW had a great deal of history in the United States in the mid-1990s, but few new car sales. Volkswagen models that sold well in Europe did not catch on across the Atlantic. The factory was searching for the answer to the American sales dilemma. *Volkswagen of America*

The New Beetle was created on paper in the mid-1990s. As the idea was refined, the arched design of the original was retained. *Volkswagen of America*

After production ceased many, many Bugs continued to roam the roads. In fact, of all of the "old" cars running, there may be more Bugs being driven than any other make. The United States is full of very active clubs, supported by a large aftermarket parts community. Some at Volkswagen felt that this popularity would give them an upper hand in marketing a new Bug. Others thought "Oh no, not again."

The first battle for the new Beetle would not be on the showroom floors competing with other automakers. The first battle for those in favor of resurrecting the Bug would be to sway the skeptical minds that inhabit any large automotive manufacturer. Within the employee and management communities of the Volkswagen Corporation, there have always been mixed opinions about the Bug. For most VW employees, the Bug was a car they were stuck with. It came into being after the war, and it was a car that Germans and other Europeans had to put up with until their economies were rebuilt. Many of the factory workers didn't like the car because while the rest of the world's auto companies were working on new, flashy, powerful designs, they were refining an underpowered, uncomfortable, slow, ill-handling car. Even in the early 1990s, some still had this attitude.

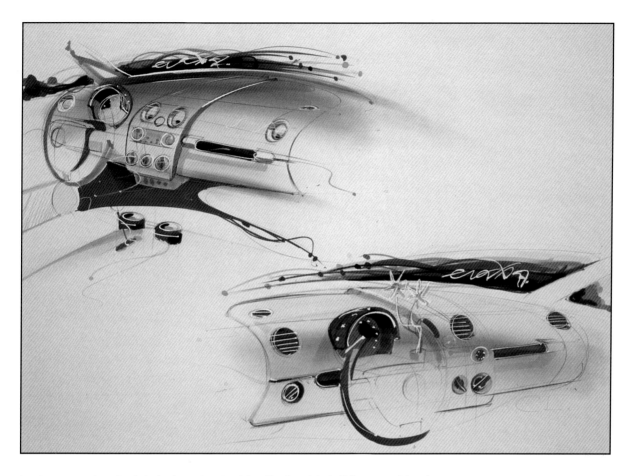

Interior concepts kept the dash simple yet functional, just like the original. *Volkswagen of America*

But those who wanted to bring it back had a few things going for them. First of all, as the 1990s began, things were far from rosy for Volkswagen in the American market. In 1970, Volkswagen sold over a half-million cars in the United States. But by 1992 this number was down to 40,000 cars, representing the combined sales of the Golf, the Passat, and the Jetta. The truth was that Volkswagen was in great jeopardy of becoming extinct in the U.S. market. Sales of the VW lines were so dismal that the factory in Pennsylvania built to produce them for the U.S. market was closed. Golf sales in Europe were strong, but the competitive car market of the United

States proved to be too much for the model. Unlike Europe, the United States was making minivans and SUVs the mainstream of the automobile market. In America, the price of fuel remained substantially lower than in most European countries, allowing Americans to still indulge their habit of driving large cars, or small cars with big engines. If the American buyer went with an import, chances are it would be a Honda, Toyota, Nissan, BMW, or Mercedes. This critical sales and marketing situation was possibly the biggest asset the new Bug project had going for it. If the North American operation had been highly profitable, it is doubtful

After a design was selected, the car went from paper to clay. Volkswagen engineers sculpted a model by hand, with the help of computer-controlled measuring devices. *Volkswagen of America*

Finally the car went from clay to prototype, and the Concept 1 actually existed. The car would be introduced to the world at the 1994 International Auto Show in Detroit, the heart of America's automotive empires. *Volkswagen of America*

the New Beetle would have made it off of the drawing board.

Even so, advocates for the New Beetle had to be very careful. The original Bug was a great car in a sense different from your average great car. The Bug's greatness was achieved not from mechanical superiority or personal comfort, but for affording freedom at a low price and sometimes as a political statement. Many connected the Bug with youth, adventure, and just being different. In the 1960s the Bug was a counterstatement to the establishment's big, comfortable, gas-guzzling sedans. But the 1990s were different from the 1960s. Many things that the factory did to make the car inexpensive could not be repeated, due to tighter laws. There are many more regulations for safety, pollution, and so on. Production of the original Bug for the U.S. market ended primarily because of new standards for both crash safety and engine emissions. The main culprits were the National Highway Safety Act of 1966 and the Clean Air Act of 1970, both of which impacted the Bug heavily. With a rear engine and a relatively light body, the Bug was not exceptionally safe, especially in head-on collisions. Plus, the original Bug was a low-dollar purchase, and affordability will always be a big selling point for any product. If the car were burdened with more costly items, such as 5-mile per hour bumpers, air bags, and air conditioning, the price would go up. The car's weight would go up, which meant it would be slower or the factory would have to increase horsepower. If the factory opted for the

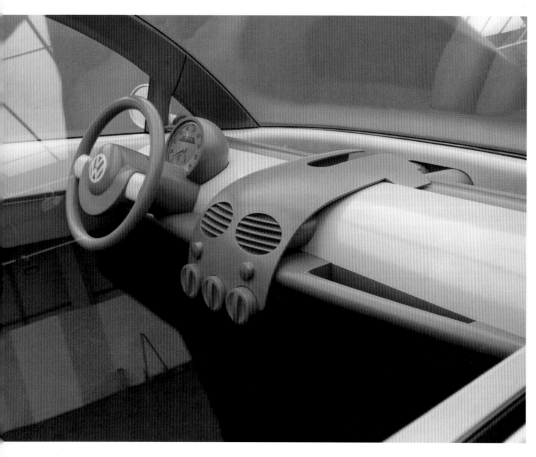

While the prototypes were different (quite a bit, actually) from the final production car, they did do a good job of illustrating what was to come. *Volkswagen of America*

Interior appointments on the new car were much like the prototype—simple and functional. With excellent heating and air conditioning, trips in the New Beetle seemed much shorter than with the old car.

latter, more costs would have be absorbed by VW or passed on to its customers.

Another possible problem with the new Bug was the stiffer competition in world automobile markets. Many factories in Asia, Europe, and America were producing powerful, high-quality automobiles, and consumers had many more models to choose from. Customers' buying habits had changed. There was the booming sale of sport utility vehicles. In the 1950s, 1960s, and 1970s,

SUVs were mainly driven by hunters and forest rangers, but they were now being commanded by country club wives. In America, big and roomy was the choice of adults, and small and shiny was the choice of the youth. (Which small and shiny didn't matter, as long as it had a huge stereo.)

And finally there was the link to the original Bug. A "bring-back" car model is like making a sequel to a movie. It's a risky proposition, especially if the original is very well remembered by the public.

If the Bug was brought back as a rather expensive, technologically advanced platform, would the public be offended? I love the movie *Rocky*, and Rocky *II* wasn't too bad, but *III*, *IV*, and *V*? Give me a break. It's an obvious attempt to cash in on the artistic value of the first movie with cheap thrills and dreams of box-office cash returns. Some at Volkswagen felt that the public might have a similar reaction to the resurrection of the Bug. After all, if you have spent much time around Bug people, you know that many of them view any deviation from the original as a blasphemy. If a new Bug were to hit the market, would Bug enthusiasts be pleased or offended? This was the next battle that had to be won for the New Beetle to be successful. Would a modern version of a 50-year-old design sell, especially since the new car would be dramatically different from the original? But the first battle to be fought would be waged within the corporate halls of headquarters.

All the commotion about a new Beetle was a reaction to two guys in California who had an idea. Resurrection of the Bug began in 1991, with a project that would be known as Concept 1. Credit for getting the ball rolling is generally given to J. Mays and Freeman Thomas. Mays was the head of a new Volkswagen design center, the Simi Valley Design Studio, located in California. Thomas was his chief designer. In the early 1990s, Mays and German designer Peter Schreyer, who was visiting the Simi Valley studio, had conversations about the difficulties in North American VW sales. They realized that one of the great difficulties in selling VW Golfs, Passats, and Jettas was that when an American heard the name Volkswagen, or the letters VW, the linked image was, and probably would always be, the Bug. This was an overwhelming challenge and handicap in new product marketing.

Later, back at the shop, Mays discussed this topic with Freeman Thomas. Mays and Thomas had similar careers and similar backgrounds, and though both were Americans, each had a stint working in Germany. The big question was whether this emotionally linked image could become an asset to sales instead of a liability.

Although it is easy to now call the New Beetle a brilliant success, the two men had a treacherous path ahead. Before design and engineering could be considered, Mays and Thomas had to negotiate the political system of a large international company for permission and funding. As Mays has said, it took three days to design the car, but years to sell it. The fact that Volkswagen was not doing well in the United States offered advantages, but also a potential hazard to those who dreamed of a new Bug. With sales and profitability lagging, the higher-ups in management would probably be receptive to any new idea that would increase sales. However, the same conditions would make it difficult to find money for design, testing, and retooling. working up their initial rough proposal for the New Beetle, Mays and Thomas sent it to Hartmut Warkuss, the design director for the entire Volkswagen group at Volkswagen AG. Warkuss was intrigued and wanted to see the project further developed, but with little exposure. The next step for the pro-Bug group would be to sell the idea to Ferdinand Piech.

The project was somewhat slowed when, in 1992, Thomas went to Audi, VW's sister company. While there he still played with the new Bug designs on his own time. In late 1992, Warkuss gave permission for two quarter-scale models to be produced. The project was slowly moving from paper to model, although at this point, the planned use for the designs and models was unclear. In a way the idea's advancement was to some degree based on a lie. In order to get the project going, the designers associated it with a movement to meet future U.S. government requirements. Primarily, they used California's new law, which mandated that by 1998 (later changed to 2002), two percent of all manufacturers' sales would consist of zero-emissions cars. The designers proposed the car under the premise that it would be produced to meet this state requirement. As it was being proposed as an electric car, the model was often referred to as the "Lightning Bug."

The designers wanted the car to have the pleasing and distinctive lines of the original car, but

No longer would owners go to the back to check the engine in their Beetles. Based on the Golf chassis, the New Beetle was much more conventional than its predecessor.

with its own identity. It was decided to not blend the fenders into the body but to leave them as they were, separate bolt-on items. The new car would still have an arched roof—the designers wanted to re-create the Bug's spirit and cuteness, to make people remember the good times—but not the design and engineering of the car, which in certain areas had left much to be desired.

Mays and Thomas had different design backgrounds, and as a result their initial designs were quite different. But they could work well together, and the design gradually was refined, incorporating

Next Page
By 1999 production was catching up with demand, and more New Beetles were being seen on the street. The factory did not forget the past, and offered the New Beetle in some unique colors. No other car could carry this color and look great.

The factory paid attention to small details, and the New Beetle offered amenities that previous Beetle owners had never known. A handy eyeglass holder is located to the left of the driver, freeing up the sun visor to serve its intended purpose. *William Burt— Buster Miles Chevrolet*

the ideas of both designers. When quarter-scale models were completed, they were taken to a public beach in California to be photographed. Mays and Thomas presented the models and other concepts for the cars to Warkuss in early 1993.

The presentation was successful, and it was sent to Germany to be presented to Piech. He was also enthusiastic and gave the go-ahead for the development process to continue. The project would proceed with the title Concept 1.

While the initial concept was generated in California, the work now shifted to Germany and specifically to Rudiger Folten, who would lead the project. Some at Volkswagen in Germany were not enthusiastic about the prospect of a new Bug, but many did see the Concept 1 as a good platform to introduce some of their new engines to the press. The car might draw enough attention that members of the press would listen to the presentation about

the new engines—a direct injection diesel with a turbo; a diesel electric engine, much like a U-boat; and a purely electric engine.

The first public test for the project would be the North American International Auto Show, to be held in Detroit in 1994. There, a huge contingency from the automotive press would be assembled in the heart of the American market. If the new Bug generated a lot of interest at the show, and thus with the press, it would give the car a much better chance of going into production. The Concept 1 project was held in incredibly tight secrecy leading up to the show. Unless you were very close to the project, and already "in the know," you weren't allowed anywhere near the car. Even the head of Audi, Volkswagen's sister company, was denied an early peek at the car. When it was finally rolled to its display area, it was covered with Styrofoam blocks and tarps to prevent any early looks.

When Volkswagen officials took them off and the automotive press got a good look, Volkswagen knew that it had a hit.

The great reception at the Detroit Auto Show led to approval in November of 1994 to produce the New Beetle. The emotional part of the game was over. Both the public and Volkswagen management seemed to be behind the car. Now the focus would be on making a profitable venture of the new Bug. This would be the second major battle.

The car would compete in a tough market, a market very different from the one in which the original Bug thrived. The original Bug was a great, inexpensive car. (OK, it was downright cheap.) In the mid-1990s in the United States, the competition among inexpensive cars was intense. Cars like Chrysler's new Neon were priced at less than $10,000, and many other Asian and American companies offered comparable deals. Could the new Bug compete in the same market? If the car were more expensive (a great possibility due to the low sales forecast), would it drive buyers away? The best guess for the new Bug sales was around 100,000 units a year worldwide, with half of these aimed toward American roads.

While the new car would share the same general shape as the original car, it would really be vastly different. The original Bug was rear-wheel drive; the New Beetle would be front-wheel drive. The original Bug's engine was in the rear; in the New Beetle, the engine would be in the front. The original Bug had an air-cooled engine; the New Beetle's engine would be water cooled. In addition, the New Beetle would have air conditioning, power steering, power brakes, a computer-controlled engine, power windows, and air bags, none of which were offered on the original Bug.

By 1995 a drivable prototype was ready, and the results were not grand. After Volkswagen Chairman Ferdinand Piech personally drove the car, neither he nor anyone else was pleased, especially with the handling. Piech did not want to build the car just to have a new Bug. The car would have to embody the quality and characteristics of all Volkswagen products. If the car could not, it would not be built. Thus, with the specter of higher development and production costs, the feelings were not as rosy as they had been the previous year. The project was in jeopardy of being canceled.

Enter the "Golf connection." In the mid 1990s, Volkswagen was selling about three-quarters of a million Golfs a year worldwide. While the car never had great success in America, it did very, very well in Europe. It was a tried and true automotive platform. The problem was that the Golf was undergoing a redesign in the mid-1990s, to be introduced in 1998. This stressed the design and manufacturing capabilities of VW and made the proposition of developing a New Beetle at the same time a stretch for the company.

So the factory guys proposed an economical solution. To ease the development and production costs of the New Beetle, the car was redesigned to utilize the basic Golf platform. The factory would use as many of the tried and true parts of the Golf as possible to build the Bug. This would have quite an impact on the car, especially related to the initial Concept 1 project. It meant the production Bug would be bigger than the Concept 1. The wheelbase would grow by over 6 inches (from 92.1 to 98.9 inches). The production car's overall length would grow by almost a foot. The width of the car would grow from 65.1 inches to 67.9 inches. The biggest change was the increase in weight. Concept 1 clocked in at a very lean 1,430 pounds while the "Golf platform" Bug weighed 2,712 pounds.

One danger that was still lurking was the sales price. Many feared that when the dust settled there would be no way to sell the new Bug for less than the Golf, and most felt that for the Bug to sell, it would have to remain a relatively inexpensive choice. The selling price fear was based primarily on the estimated production runs, 100,000 Bugs versus 700,000 Golfs. The in-house factory design teams were quite busy with the redesign of the Golf, so much of the development work for the New Beetle was subcontracted, or it took second seat to the Golf. But basing the New Beetle body on the Golf chassis saved critical funds in development and tooling. Plus, with the increased size, the car would be more comfortable.

The New Beetle has a surprisingly large trunk. For short trips, four people can travel comfortably. With only two passengers, the rear seats can be folded to carry a great deal more luggage. *William Burt—Buster Miles Chevrolet*

Everything seems backward on the new Beetle. Fuel is added in the rear, while the engine is in the front. *William Burt— Buster Miles Chevrolet*

The Golf and the New Beetle would share the same hard points and the same seat locations. They would both be offered with either a 2.0-liter, four-cylinder gas or a 1.9-liter turbo diesel, which were both Golf engines. They also had the same five-speed manual or four-speed automatic transmission. The New Beetle and the Golf shared steering and basic suspension components, although the New Beetle did have a different rear spring setup. Under its skin, the New Beetle would be about 80 percent Golf.

Finally the New Beetle was ready to go to the show. The last show car before production was unveiled at the Geneva Motor Show in 1996. Again the car was well received, but it wasn't quite finished. In late 1997 one of the final battles to be fought was over the new car's brakes. The car had been developed with drum brakes on all four wheels to keep cost as low as possible. This was something not seen in America on a new production car for many years, and it was a problem for Ferdinand Piech. He wanted disc brakes, and just

before the car went into production he got his wish. The car would roll off the assembly line with 11-inch vented discs in the front and 9.4-inch solid discs in the rear.

The New Beetle had finally arrived. The production version of the New Beetle was introduced in Detroit in January 1998. The car was announced to have a base price of $15,220—not cheap, but well under $20,000. True, you could buy a less expensive car, but the $10,000 cars usually lacked both personality and refinement. The $15,000 range in America was the entry-level price for cars with personality, so the new Bug's pricing fit the market nicely.

What did the buyer get for a little over 15 grand? Dimensionally the New Beetle would have a wheelbase of 98.9 inches, a width of 67.9 inches, a length of 161.1 inches, and a height of 59.5 inches. Under the hood, the car would have either a 2.0-liter inline four-cylinder engine, rated at 115 horsepower and capable of pulling the car from 0 to 60 in 10.5 seconds, or a 1.9-liter diesel turbo

Getting behind the wheel of a New Beetle with a turbo and a five-speed is a thrilling experience. This model best illustrates the tremendous engineering gap between the original Beetle and the new car. The car is quick to accelerate, has acceptable top-end power, and handles quite well. The efficiency of the four-wheel disc brakes helps the car decelerate as well as it accelerates. *William Burt— Buster Miles Chevrolet*

rated at 90 horsepower (and 149 ft-lb torque with a 0–60 speed in the 13-second range. The gas engine was rated at 31 miles per gallon and the diesel at 48 miles per gallon. The diesel was a $1,275 option, but would pay for itself at the pump. Since both available engines got fuel from a 14.5-gallon fuel tank, the car's range was 449 miles for the gas engine and 696 miles for the diesel. The car would slow from 60 to 0 in 155 feet.

Standard equipment on the new Bug included 16-inch wheels with 205/55R16H tires; front and side air bags; four-wheel disc brakes; power steering, with a rack and pinion; vinyl or cloth seats; an alarm system; power locks; a radio and cassette stereo; CFC-free air conditioning; and an air filtration system. Volkswagen also gave customers a full-size spare tire.

If a customer didn't mind a little larger sticker price, options included a CD player, cruise control, leather seats, seat heaters, a leather steering wheel, a leather shift knob, power windows, a power sunroof, and ABS brakes. Most of the first cars to the dealers had a few options and were sticker-priced at $16,000

to $17,000, but the cars were selling for more. The great initial demand for cars allowed dealers to charge more than sticker price. It was the beginning that Volkswagen had hoped for.

Where will it end? It is doubtful that the New Beetle will ever achieve the popularity of the original Bug. And don't lose sight of the fact that the New Beetle is 80 percent Golf, a car that was never enormously popular among American buyers. By the nature of its development, the New Beetle can never be seen as a completely unique car, as the original Bug can.

Perhaps it is best to see the New Beetle as a tribute to three different entities. First, to the company that did such a fine job creating and producing the most popular car in history. Second, to the Bug itself, which was so resilient throughout its production life and even after its production death. And third, to the tremendously loyal army of Bug fanatics who, through their care and love, have kept so many Bugs alive and well throughout the past 60 years.

Long live the Bug!

INDEX

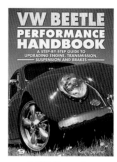